# Eyes View

## A Collection Of Poetry
### By Torrilorri

# Table Of Contents

1. Dedication----------------------------------------4
2. Forward-------------------------------------------5
3. Father And Daughter----------------------------6
4. Monster-------------------------------------------8
5. The Path------------------------------------------10
6. Basketball----------------------------------------12
7. The Bravest--------------------------------------17
8. I Am Through------------------------------------20
9. Depression---------------------------------------22
10. Where I'm Set Free----------------------------24
11. Because Of You--------------------------------26
12. Lost-----------------------------------------------28
13. Heaven-------------------------------------------30
14. I Dare You---------------------------------------32
15. Demons------------------------------------------34
16. Life------------------------------------------------36
17. I'm The One-------------------------------------38
18. Pain-----------------------------------------------40
19. Someone-----------------------------------------42
20. Reflection Of You------------------------------44
21. Is There?-----------------------------------------46
22. Clearing Haze-----------------------------------48
23. Invading------------------------------------------50
24. Bare Dungeon----------------------------------52
25. Rain Beat Drum--------------------------------54
26. No One-------------------------------------------56
27. Lost Lamb---------------------------------------58
28. Acid Rain-----------------------------------------60
29. Our Own Fight---------------------------------64
30. The World's Darkest Day--------------------67
31. Hymn Icarus------------------------------------68
32. Punctured Puppeteer-------------------------70
33. Chaos Before The Calm----------------------72
34. Henri----------------------------------------------74
35. Soundless Scream-----------------------------78
36. Grand Plans-------------------------------------80
37. Evan-----------------------------------------------82
38. 24 Years Old------------------------------------84
39. In-Between--------------------------------------86
40. Silent Serenade--------------------------------88
41. Meet You There--------------------------------90
42. Chorus Of Angels-----------------------------92
43. All You See--------------------------------------94

# Table Of Contents

44. Self-Created---------------------------------------96
45. Angels Dwell---------------------------------------98
46. Hue Of Blue---------------------------------------100
47. Short Season--------------------------------------102
48. Magnificent Red Marble-----------------------104
49. Temperant------------------------------------------108
50. Henri's Heightening-----------------------------110
51. Mimic------------------------------------------------112
52. Starboard Soul-----------------------------------114
53. Torri's Story---------------------------------------116
54. Riddled---------------------------------------------118
55. Wandering Soul----------------------------------122
56. Elivia------------------------------------------------124
57. Binder-----------------------------------------------128

# Dedication

This book is dedicated to ***all*** who are ***lost, outcast, or weird***
You are important, you are not alone, and you have a purpose.
Don't let the darkness of this world frighten you when the light
you need to guide your way is **<u>found within your own soul</u>**.

# Forward

Poetry has always been a part of my soul. It was not something introduced to me at an early age, other than my father reading Dr Seuss before bed. Our favorite was Hop on Pop and by 3 years old I would change the words to "No No Pat! Don't sit on that!" when Pat would go to sit on the cactus. Things made more sense to me when rhyming was involved. I would often create stanzas in my head and recite them to bring me comfort. Poetry was never something I needed instructions to know how to do. For me it came as easily as breathing. It was simply a part of me.

I was off to the races with my poetry once I learned to write. I was 11 years old in 2004 while in the 5th grade and had easily written a hundred poems by that point. I had even been published in A Celebration of Young Poets-South Spring 2004, using my poem "Father And Daughter" which is featured on the next page. My mother told me if I was to continue writing I should begin to sign and date each poem so I could appreciate them in the years to come. My father bought me my very first 2-inch binder to keep my poems safe. Little did we know at the time how that binder would overflow with poems as the years passed.

Eyes View has been the epitome of how I always envisioned my poetry reaching the public. Most poems in this collection also have a scanned copy of the original poem after the typed copy. As my poetry has evolved so has my mind and especially my emotions. Reading through my original, hand-written poems, my state-of-mind is evident and easily recognized by my handwriting. It has always mirrored my emotion throughout every phase of my life. I could have two poems written on the same day in different handwritings because one poem may have been written out of rage while the other poem written out of anguish.

This collection has been placed in chronological order to give the reader an open invitation to experience how my mind as well as my emotions have developed from the age of 11 to 30. This book will take you through all my ups and downs, victories and failures, including pivotal life moments that shaped me. Eyes View is a visceral account of my life. I have hand selected each of these 55 poems to show all sides of my life; the good, the bad, and the gray in between.

I used to question why I always felt emotions so heavily and displayed them so publicly. But I've come to the realization that without these transparent emotions, my life would have taken a different route and poetry may not have been a part of that. I know from experience how heavy and debilitating the low emotions can be, but I also know how light and freeing the higher emotions are as well. Without the dark we would need no light, and without the pain we would seek no comfort. I hope this reaches you and gives you the strength to continue your fight, because brighter days are sure to follow, just as a beautiful rainbow follows a dark storm.

# Father And Daughter

Sometimes I think you don't like me anymore this is very true
Sometimes I think you don't like me anymore and I just don't know what to do
    You yell and scream
    And though it seems
    That sometimes you're just so mean
I know that I can be really bad sometimes
But I really do try to be kind
    I'll kick and yell and scream and hit
    But I'm not trying to throw a fit
But when it gets to the end you'll be my father and I'll be your daughter
And something like this will go even farther
    I'll hug and kiss when it gets to the end
    But something like us will never end
I hope you understand what I am trying to say
I'm saying that I love you even more every single day

                    TORRiLORRi
                    2004ish
            Dedicated to my father, Rob Hebert

# Father And Daughter

# Monster

There's a monster under my bed with sharp yellow teeth
It scares me from my head down to my feet
    Crawling around my room in the middle of the night
    Waiting 'til the time is right
To steal my candy and my toys
It's the monster of the 3 lil' boys
    It's their dog and his name is monster
    He runs so fast he sounds like thunder
So if you think there's a monster under your bed and you don't know what to do
Just throw a dog treat out your door and he won't bother you!

                    TORRiLORRi
                    2004ish

# Monster

Monster

There's a monster under my bed w/ sharp yello teeth
It scares me from my head down to my feet
Crawling around my room in the middle of the night
Waiting til' the time is right
To steel my candy and my toys
Its the monster of the 3 lil' boys
Its their dog and his name is monster
He runs so fast he sounds like thunder
So if you think theres a monster under your bed and
you don't know what to do
Just throw a dog treat out your door and he
won't bother you

By: Torri Hebert
2004ish

# The Path

It's the path to God
    The one all of us should take
The path of honor and courage
    To the one of no mistake

It's the path of the children of God
    It's the path of the all-knowing and true
It's the path to the ones we love
    And this path is just waiting for you

It's the path that can protect and save you
    Allowing you to spread your wings
Holding your hands to fly high in the sky
    The path that leads to the greatest things

Holding you up, not letting you down
    Picking you up high off your feet
Watching you become the person you are
    This path is just right down your street

This path is called heaven
    The hardest path to get through
The path of hope, love, honor, and cherish
    The path just sitting there waiting for you

TORRiLORRi
2004ish

# The Path

It's the path to God
The one all of us should take
The path of ~~a~~ honor and courage
To the one of no mistake

It's the path of the children of God
It's the path of the all-knowing and true
It's the path to the ones we love
And this path is just waiting for you

It's the path that can protect and save you
Allowing you to spread your wings
Holding your hands to fly high in the sky
The path that leads to the greatest things

Holding you up, not letting you down
Picking you up high off your feet
Watching you become the one person you are
This path is just right down your street

This path is called heaven
~~The path~~ The hardest path to get through
The path of hope, love, honor, and cherish
The path just sitting there ~~for you.~~ waiting for you.

2004ish   By: Torri Hebert

# Basketball

Her heart was just too solid
    The pace was just too fast
It was the hardest game of her life
    She didn't know if she would last

The hour was getting shorter
    Her time was running out
Their score was very low
    She thought they'd lose without a doubt

They were in the 4$^{th}$ quarter
    There were 2 minutes left on the clock
She looked up for a second
    And her friend had made a shot

Now the pressure was on
    The score was tied
With 58 seconds left
    They could not let them get by

The other team had the ball
    So they took it in
This was their last chance
    They could not go back again

Blair had made an incredible steal
    With 10 seconds left on the clock
She passed the ball to me
    And I had made the shot

The buzzer went off
    We had won the championship game
We got t-shirts and trophies
    We had all the glory and fame

# Basketball

I went to bed that night
      With the game rolling around in my head
I couldn't sleep
      Because all I could think about was what you said

You told me to always follow my dreams
      When I was just a kid
You told me to follow my heart
      So that is what I did

We might have played hard
      We might have won the game
We might have beat the other teams
      One day we might even play in the WNBA

You've always believed in me
      You always said I could
You never gave up on me
      And I never thought you would

So thanks Mom and Dad
      Yes, I love you too
I would have never made it this far
      I would have never won without you

                TORRiLORRi
                2004ish
                For Sylvia and Rob Hebert

# Basketball

Her heart was just to solid
The pace was just to fast
It was the hardest game of her life
She didn't know if she would last

The hour was getting shorter
Her time was running out
Their score was very low
She thought they'd lose without a doubt

They were in the 4th quarter
There were 2 minutes left on the clock
She looked up for a second
And her friend had made a shot

Now the preasure was on
The score was tied
With 58 seconds left
They could not let them get by

The other team had the ball
So they took it in
This was their last chance
They could not go back again

# Basketball

Blair had made an incredible steal
With 10 seconds left on the clock
She passed the ball to me
And I had made the shot

The buzzer went off
We had won the chamionship game
We got T-shirts and trophies
We had all the glory and fame

I went to bed that night
With the game rolling around in my head
I couldn't sleep
B/c all I could think about was what you said

You told me to always follow my dreams
When I was just a kid
You told me to follow my heart
So that is what I did

We might have played hard
We might have won the game
We might have beat the other teams
One day we might even play in the WNBA

# Basketball

You've always believed in me
You always said I could
You never gave up on me
And I never thought you would

So thanks Mom and Dad
Yes I love you too
I would have never made it this far
I would have never won without you

By: Torri Hebert
For: Sylvia and Rob Hebert
So Thanks Mom and Dad
2004ish

# The Bravest

Why am I here, why are they gone
Why am I the one that gets to go home
    They had a family, they had loved ones too
    I feel so guilty, what am I to do?
When I'm in a crowded room I feel so alone
But when I'm by myself I feel like I'm home
    They risked everything they had for people they didn't even know
    People call me brave but they are the ones that had the bravery to show
The firefighters and police officers that left everything behind
To save all those people are going down in time
    On 9/11 was the day that I let everything go and began to cry
    I was young but I knew what was wrong and what was right
Are you going to go home and watch that violent show on TV
Or are you going to sit on your bed and put yourself out of your misery
    Just think about all those children who lost everything they used to have
    Think of that mom with her baby girl crying out to God, "Why did you take her Dad?"
I can tell my children I saw the bravest people on Earth go down in flames
I'll tell them how I cried and I knew nothing would ever be the same
    You wouldn't believe what the burning fire and the darkness of the smoke could do to your soul
    It can change you and make you feel something you can't control
I know they are helping us, and I know they are being brave
But how can you leave your family just to go to an early grave
    Take pride in your country because those men and women put everything on the line
    They are the bravest souls you will ever know and they will be remembered in time

TORRiLORRi
4/18/2005
In memory of all who lost their life during 9/11/2001

# The Bravest

Why am I here, why are they gone so into now?
Why am I the one that gets to go home to something
They had a family, they had loved ones too
I feel so guilty, what am I to do?
When I'm in a crowded room I feel so alone
But when I'm by myself I feel like I'm home
They risked everything they had for people they didn't even know
People call me brave but they are the ones that had the bravery to show
The firefighters + police officers that left everything behind
To save all those people are going down in time
On 9/11 was the day that I let everything go + began to cry
I was young but I knew what was wrong + what was right
Are you going to go home + watch that violent show on TV
Or are you going to sit on your bed + put yourself out of your misery
Just think about all those children who lost everything they used to have
Think of that mom with her baby girl crying out to God "Why did you take her dad?"
I can tell my children I saw the bravest people on Earth go down in flames
I'll tell them how I cried + I knew nothing would ever be the same

# The Bravest

You wouldn't belive what the burning of the fire and the darkness of the smoke could do to your soul

It can change you & make you feel something you can't control.

I know they are helping us, and I know they are being brave

But how can you leave your family just to go to an early grave

Take pride in you country b/c those men and women put everything on the line

They are the bravest soul you will ever know and they will be remembered in time.

By: Torri Hebert
April 18, 2005

In rememberance of everyone who risked everything on 9/11/01

# I Am Through

The worrying that's inside
The problems I can't deny
    The rumors going around
    That evil, vicious sound
Of kids laughing at me
The hurting no one can see
    Laughing and teasing and so much more
    I am the one that no one adores
These things are getting in
Deep inside my skin
    Down to my heart
    My world's falling apart
All because of you
I have no idea what to do
    You've tormented and teased and everything in between
    All those smiles that people give aren't what they seem
Laughing at me, showing no respect
You're a jerk but who am I to suspect
    So leave me alone, get it through your head
    And just be quiet because you've hurt me with everything you've said
So I'm done with this, I'm done with you
Leave me alone, I am through

        TORRiLORRi
        11/3/2005

# I Am Through

I am through
The worrying that's inside
The problems I can't deny
The rumors going around
That evil, vicious sound
Of kids laughing at me
The hurting no one can see
Laughing and teasing and so much more
I am the one that no one adores
These things are getting in
Deep inside my skin
Down to my heart
My world's falling apart
All because of you
I have no idea what to do
You've tormented and teased an everything in between
All those smiles that people give aren't what they seem
Laughing at me, showing no respect
You're a jerk but who am I to suspect
So leave me alone, get it through your head
And just be quiet because you've hurt me with everything you've said
So I'm done with this I'm done with you
Leave me alone, I am through

By: Torri Hebert
11/3/05

# Depression

Depression
Obsession
    It's what I'm living by
Living
And giving
    The rumors I can't deny
In pain
The same
    As I was before
I have shame
And I'm taking the blame
    For sure
Deceiving
Intriguing
    It's all put into one
Superstitions
Decisions
    Should I fire that gun?
Upset
Regret
    There's too much to go around
Denial
On trial
    There's too much crime in this town
I'm finished
You win it
    You beat me fair in square
Jesus
Please lead us
    To someone who really cares

TORRiLORRi
11/2/2005

# Depression

Depression
Obsession
It's what I'm living by
Living
And giving...
The rumors I can't deny
In pain
The same
As I was before
I have shame
And I'm taking the blame
For sure
Deceiving
Intriging
It's all put into one
Superstition
Decisions
Should I fire that gun?
Upset
Regret
There's too much to go around
Denile
On trial
There's too much crime in this town
I'm finished
You win it

You beat me fair in square
Jesus
Please lead us
To someone who really cares

By: Torri Hebert
1/2/05

# Where I'm Set Free

Neglect
Regret
    This is what I feel
Abuse
The truth
    Is none of this real?
Away
Today
    Where everything's the same
No hate
No fate
    But only just a game
Ridicule
And fools
    Are never found here
Love
From above
    Is always held dear
In our hearts
Our world's falling apart
    But no one will listen to us say
What we feel
When nothing's real
    Because we're broken every single day
In our minds
Is where we find
    How we want our life to be
Letting go
For you to know
    That's where I'm set free

TORRiLORRi
11/3/2005

# Where I'm Set Free

Where I'm Set Free
Neglect
Regret
This is what I feel
Abuse
The truth
Is none of this is real
Aways
Today
Where everything's the same
No hate
No fate
But only just a game
Ridicule
And fools
Are never found here
Love
From Above
Is always held dear
In our hearts
Our world's falling apart
But no one will listen to us say
What we feel
When nothing's real
Because we're broken every single day
In our minds
Is where we find

How we want our life to be
Letting go
For you to know
That's where I'm set free

By: Torri Hebert
IV 3/05

# Because Of You

Screaming hearts
Falling apart
    I don't know what to do
Shattered dreams
Tattered seams
    I don't know if I love you
I know it hurts
Through these words
    That I'm speaking of
I know it's real
The way I feel
    But is it truly love
Hurting inside
I can't deny
    That you're really gone
Seeing these
Pieces of me
    I don't know where they're coming from
Real life
Tonight
    Is only fun and games
To give
To live
    Things just aren't the same
Mended thoughts
Battles fought
    So I could be with you
And then the world
Begins to twirl
    Because I have you
I was confused
Intruged
    By what you did and have done
I don't know how
But right now
    I have won
I won the game
That I tried to play
    But I couldn't make it through
I only made it
I only faded
    Because of you

TORRiLORRi
11/11/2005

# Because Of You

Because of you
Screaming hearts
Falling apart
I don't know what to do
Shattered dreams
Tattered seams
I Don't know if I love you
I know it hurts
Through these words
That I'm speaking of
I know it's real
The way I feel
But is it truely love
Hurting inside
I can't deny
That you're really gone
Seeing these
Pieces of me
I don't know where they're coming from
Real life
Tonight
Is only fun and games
To give
To live
Things just aren't the same
Mended thoughts
Battles fought
So I could be with you
And then the world
Begins to twirl
Because I have you
I was confused
Intrueged
By what you did and have done
I don't know how
But right now
I have won
I won the game
That I tried to play
But I couldn't make it through
I only made it
I only faded
Because of you

By Jorey Hebert
11/11/05

# Lost

Cutting
Shutting
    You out of my life
Hoping
Knowing
    That nothing is alright
Crying
And hiding
    Under my tears
Hating
Stating
    No one is near
And lying
Not fighting
    Against the devil in me
But worrying
Is only hurting
    The one I want to be
I'm young
And from
    The bravest of them all
But I
Can't deny
    That compared to them I just fall
These years
Are here
    Hurting and crying at night
We're lost
In thoughts
    And still thinking nothing will be alright

                TORRiLORRi
                12/13/2005

# Lost

Lost
Cutting
Shutting
You out of my life
Hoping
Knowing
That nothing is alright
Crying
And Hiding
Under my tears
Hurting
Stating
No one is near
And lying
Not fighting
Against the devil in me
But worrying
Is only hurting
The one I want to be
I'm young
And from
The bravest of them all
But I
Can't deny
That compared to them I just fall
These years
Are here
Hurting and crying at night
We're lost
In thoughts
And still thinking nothing will be alright

By: Torri Hebert
12/13/05

# Heaven

Let me fly,
Up so high
    Spread my wings and leave this place
Let me go
So I will know
    I am ready to fly away
Soar so long
Leaving home
    Being free in the sky
Racing you
Chasing you
    Open up and fly
It's so beautiful
And it's so wonderful
    Like nothing you've ever seen before
Up in heaven
With a grin
    You know you just want to soar
Come up here now
I'll show you how
    To live by what is right
I'm calling you
You aren't through
    But I've already seen the light

TORRiLORRi
1/10/2006

# Heaven

Heaven

Let me fly,
Go so high,
Spread my wings and leave this
　　place
Let me go
So I will know
I am ready to fly away
Soar so long
Leaving home
Being free in the sky
Racing you
Chasing you
Open up and fly
It's so beautiful
And it's so wonderful
Like nothing you've ever seen before
Up in heaven
With a grin
You know you just want to soar
Come up here now
I'll show you how
To live by what is right
I'm calling you
You aren't through
But I've already seen the light

By iTucki Herbert 1/10/06

# I Dare You

I dare you to laugh
    I dare you to hate
I dare you to hurt
    It's all too late
I dare you to look
    And I dare you to stare
I dare you to point
    When you think nothing's there
Even though I'm standing
    In the spot you're pointing to
You think I don't exist
    Come on, laugh at me more, I dare you
If you think I don't mind
    Well you're so wrong
It's bothering me
    It has all along
Just because someone tells you something
    Don't follow what they say
Set your own rules
    Don't be afraid
I'm going to forgive you
    For everything you've done to me
Just because I dare you to hate
    Doesn't mean that's who you have to be

TORRiLORRi
1/17/2006

# I Dare You

I Dare You
I dare you to laugh
I dare you to hate
I dare you to hurt
It's all too late
I dare you to look
And I dare you to stare
I dare you to point
When you think nothing's there
Even though I'm standing
In the spot you're pointing to
You think I don't exist
Come on, laugh at me more, I dare you
If you think I don't mind
Well you're so wrong
It's bothering me
It has all along
Just because someone tells you to do something
Don't follow what they say
Set your own rules
Don't be afraid
I'm going to forgive you
For everything you've done to me
Just because I dare you to hate
Doesn't mean that's who you have to be
   By: Torri Hebert
    1/17/06

# Demons

I don't like this
    Having a broken heart
And I don't like this,
    My world's falling apart
I used to be so happy
    I had so many friends
My life is so confusing
    I have no where that will end
Every day I'm starting over
    A new problem will always arise
And I will try to defeat them
    Because beneath my soul is where they lie
I'm trying to fight the demons
    The demons that torment my soul
They're the devil's little messengers
    They're there with no love to show
And I can hear the echoes
    That aren't meant to be there
I can feel the demons
    Deep inside their lair
But I will fight so hard
    Because this was not meant to be true
If I have to fight forever
    Then that is what I'll do!

TORRiLORRi
2/1/2006

# Demons

I don't like this,
Having a broken heart
And I don't like this,
My world's falling apart
I used to be so happy
I had so many friends
My life is so confusing
I have no where that will end
Every day I'm starting over
A new problem will always arise
And I will try to defeat them
Because beneath my soul is where they lie
I'm trying to fight the demons
The demons that torment my soul
They're the devils little messengers
They're there with no love to show
And I can here the echoes
That aren't ment to be there
I can feel the demons
Deep inside this lair
But I will fight so hard
Because this was not ment to be true
If I have to fight forever
then that is what I'll do!

By: Torri Hebert
2/11/04

# Life

It's a roller coaster
    Of a never ending dream
It's a car crash
    With innocent people's screams
It's a train wreck
    Because everything went wrong
It's just a beautiful disaster
    Because I had you all along
It's a collision
    Tire shrieks in the middle of the night
It's a broken heart
    Praying God will save your life
It's a horrific scream
    That no one else can hear
It's the monster in the closet
    That every child fears
It's an old book
    With pages torn and stained
It's the broken mirror
    Shattered from it's frame
These are all fears
    It's what we call life
These are the fears
    That haunt us in the night

TORRiLORRi
2/13/2006

# Life

Life
It's a rollercoaster
Of a never ending dream
It's a car crash
With innocent people's screams
It's a train wreck
Because everything went wrong
It's ~~a be~~ just a beautiful disaster
Because I had you all along
It's a collision
That shrieks in the middle of the night
It's a broken heart
Praying God will save your life
It's a horrific scream
That no one else can hear
It's the monsters in the closet
That every child fears
It's ~~the~~ an old book
With pages torn ~~out~~ and stained
It's the broken mirror
Shattered from it's frame
These are all fears
~~This is what we call life~~
It's what we call life
These are the fears
That haunt us in the night

By: Tokki Hebert
2/13/06

# I'm The One

I'm the one in that classroom
    Three seats away
I'm the one in the lunchroom
    With nothing to say
I'm the one in the courtyard
    With one person at my side
I'm the one under the bus port
    With nowhere left to hide
I'm the one on the field
    With not a word to be said
I'm the one on the curb
    With a face noncaring and red
I'm the one in the desk
    Too quiet to be
I'm the one on the walkway
    Wanting to be free
I'm the one on the stairs
    Without a smile to be seen
I'm the one writing this poem
    Without a mind filled of anything
I'm the one in this classroom
    Three seats away
The one that doesn't "exist"
    The one with nothing to say

TORRiLORRi
2/15/2006

# I'm The One

I'm the One
I'm the one in that classroom
Three seats away
I'm the one in the lunchroom
With nothing to say
I'm the one in the courtyard
With one person at my side
I'm the one under the bus port
With nowhere left to hide
I'm the one on the field
With not a word to be said
I'm the one on the curb
With a face uncaring and red
I'm the one in the desk
Too quiet to be
I'm the one on the walkway
Wanting to be free
I'm the one on the stairs
Without a smile to be seen
I'm the one writing this poem
Without a mind filled of anything
I'm the one in this classroom
Three seats away
The one that doesn't "exist"
The one with nothing to say

By: Torri Hebert
2/15/06

# Pain

If my life was a book
    It'd be entitled "Pain"
There'd be pages and pages
    Of nothing but change
There'd be a little girl
    Who got everything she'd ever need
But deep inside her heart
    There was only room to bleed
She never showed it
    The pain that she truly felt
She'd always hide it
    She can only play with what she's dealt
There would always be a smile on her face
    But a tear on her heart
There would always be a twinkle in her eyes
    When her world's falling apart
You would never be able to tell
    What she really felt inside
Because all of the pain and misery
    Is something she'd be able to hide
And in this book
    Of hopeless faith
Only in her heart
    Is where she'd be safe

TORRiLORRi
2/17/2006

# Pain

"Pain"

If my life was a book
It'd be entitled "Pain"
There'd be pages and pages
Of nothing but change
There'd be a little girl
Who got everything she'd ever need
But deep inside her heart
There was only room to bleed
She never showed it
The pain that she truly felt
She'd always hide it
She can only play with what she's dealt
There would always be a smile on her face
But a tore on her heart
There would always be a twinkle in her eye
When her world's falling apart
You would never be able to tell
What she really felt inside
Because all of the pain and misery
Is something she'd be able to hide
And in this book
Of hopeless faith
Only in her heart
Is where she'd be safe

By: Torri Herret
2/17/06

# Someone

If there were someone next to me
    Someone other than you
I wouldn't know where to go
    I wouldn't know what to do
And if there were someone at my side
    Someone with a different face
I wouldn't be myself
    I wouldn't be in this place
If there were someone at my right
    Someone with a different attitude
I never would have gotten this far
    I'd have a different point-of-view
If someone wouldn't push me
    And guide me along the way
I'd never make a trail
    Or a place in my heart to stay
If no one would have been there
    Or been at my side
I wouldn't want to wake up
    I'd just stay in my room, trying to hide
All I'm trying to say
    Is without you next to me
I would be completely lost
    I wouldn't know who to be

TORRiLORRi
3/1/2006

# Someone

If there were someone next to me
Someone other than you
I wouldn't know where to go
I wouldn't know what to do
And if there were someone at my side
Someone with a different face
I wouldn't be myself
I wouldn't be in this place
If there were someone at my right
Someone with a different attitude
I never would have gotten this far
I'd have a different point of view
If someone wouldn't push me
And guide me along the way
I'd never make a trail
Or a place in my heart to stay
If no one would have been there
Or been at my side
I wouldn't want to wake up
I'd just stay in my room, trying to hide
All I'm trying to say
Is without you next to me
I would be completely lost
I wouldn't know who to be.

By: Tokki Hebert
3/1/04

# Reflection Of You

Look me in the eyes
      Tell me what you see
When I look at you there's a reflection of myself
      Staring back at me
Look at me closer
      Get to know who I am
Smile at me
      And take me by the hand
Your eyes are beautiful and brown
      Mine are deep ocean blue
I don't care if we are different
      Because deep inside of me there's you
You're one that really knows me
      And guides me along the way
Hold my hand when I cry
      And makes me smile everyday
You make me happy
      I smile because you're in my life
Without you here
      Nothing would be alright
When I look in the mirror
      I'll tell you all I see
Not my reflection
      But a reflection of you, staring back at me

TORRiLORRi
3/9/2006
Dedicated to Sylvia Lorraine Hebert

# Reflection Of You

Look me in the eyes
Tell me what you see
When I look at you there's a reflection of myself
Staring back at me
Look at me closer
Get to know who I am
Smile at me
And take me by the hand
Your eyes are beautiful and brown
Mine are deep ocean blue
I don't care if we are different
Because deep inside of me there's you
You're one that really knows me
And guides me along the way
Holds my hand when I cry
And makes me smile everyday
You make me happy
I smile because you're in my life
Without you here
Nothing would be alright
When I look in the mirror
I'll tell you all I see
Not my reflection
But a reflection of you staring back at me

By: Torri Hubert
3/9/06

# Is There?

Is there something to see
Deep inside of me
Is there somewhere else to be
Besides in this dream
    Is there somewhere else to go
    Where no one else will know
    Is there something I can let go
    So I can let my real feelings show
Is there another place
Where I won't be seen in disgrace
Why can't I win this race
Or keep up with the pace
    Is there another love
    That no one is thinking of
    Or an angel up above
    To help me fly like a dove
Is there another light
Telling me to say goodnight
And giving up the fight
I had against my life
    Can the angel hear me crying
    And can the angel hear me sighing
    When deep inside I'm dying
    I have a secret, last night the angel took me flying

TORRiLORRi
3/7/2006

# Is There?

Is the something to me
Deep inside of me
Is there somewhere else to be
Besides in this dream
Is there somewhere else to go
Where noone else will know
Is there something I can let go
So I can let my real feelings show
Is there another place
Where I won't be seen in disgrace
Why can't I win this race
Or keep up with the pace
Is there another love
That noone is thinking of
Or an angel up above
To help me fly like a dove
Is there another light
Telling me to say good night
And giving up the fight
I had against my life
Can the angel hear me crying
And can the angel hear me sighing
When deep inside I'm dying
I have a secret, last night the angel took me flying

By: Torre Hebert

# Clearing Haze

I've been on this road so long
    Wandering farther and farther away
I had nowhere left to go
    And in my heart was still an empty space
Throughout my entire life
    I thought the fog would never clear
But through all the horrible weather
    You're the one that appeared
In the beginning you were only a blur
    Now I think I'm able to see
You're so close right now
    Yet, so far away from me
I've made mistakes
    Done so many things wrong
I was praying you'd come to save me
    But you were there all along
I've taken a few wrong turns
    But still, I've gone so far
Because you never gave up on me
    When I wanted to fall apart
The haze is clearing slowly
    I think you're finally in sight
I've been praying you would come
    And thank God you came tonight

TORRiLORRi
4/4/2006

# Clearing Haze

I've been on this road so long
Wandering farther and farther away
I had nowhere left to go
And in my heart was still an empty space
Throughout my entire life
I thought the fog would never clear
But through all the horrible weather
You're the one that appeared
In the beginning you were only a blur
Now I think I'm able to see
You're so close right now
Yet so far away from me
I've made mistakes,
Done so many things wrong
I was praying you'd come to save me
But you were there all along
I've taken a few wrong turns
But still, I've gone so far
Because you never gave up on me
When I wanted to fall apart
The haze is clearing slowly
I think you're finally in sight
I've been praying you would come
And thank God you came tonight

By: Torr, Herbert
4/4/09

# Invading

It's been hard
      To live the way I do
Trying to get by
      And barely getting through
I try to show a smile
      But there's tears building inside
I realize I can't always make it
      But do I always have to hide?
I doubt you can see it
      The demon invading me
The creature that crawls through my mind
      And haunts me in my sleep
It robs me from my heart
      The sweet child I used to know
Please save me from this mess
      Let my spirit go

TORRiLORRi
7/18/2006

# Invading

It's been hard
To live the way I do
Trying to get by
And barely getting through
I try to show a smile
But there's tears building inside
I realize I can't always make it
But do I have to hide
I doubt you can see it
The demon invading me
The creature that crawls through my mind
And haunts me in my sleep
It robs me from my heart
The sweet child I used to know
Please save me from this mess
Let my spirit go

By: Torri Hebert
7/18/06

# Bare Dungeon

Hiding beneath a smile
      That no one could see through
And under those ocean blue eyes
      Her feelings just couldn't pursue
Locked inside a dungeon
      Self-created and bare
Emotionally destroyed
      Locked away in despair
But how could her life come to this?
      A hole of grief and pain
It seems a fairytale to others
      But for her, it isn't the same
She's attempted letting go
      Who would care anyway
A young life left unlived
      Living one more dreaded day

TORRiLORRi
2007ish

# Bare Dungeon

Hiding beneath a smile
That no one could see through
And under those ocean blue eyes
Her feelings just couldn't pursue
Locked inside a dungion
Self created & bare
Emotionally destroyed
Locked away in dispair.

But how could her life come to this?
A note of grief & pain
It seems as a fairy tale to others
But for her, it isn't the same
She's attempted letting go
Who would care anyway
A young life left unlived
Living one more dreaded day

Tokki Lokki
2007

# Rain Beat Drum

The day was dark
      As the rain poured down
The streets were filled
      With silent sound
Deep beneath the surface
      Of that smiling, bright face
Locked away forever
      Was the innocence that she chased
Dark and dreadful
      The rain still beats
Inside the soul
      The one that weeps
Make the beating stop
      Like a silenced drum
Make the sun come out
      To show the world what it's hidden from
Uncover the mystery
      That little girl sees
Because down in her soul
      She starts to break free
She pulls from the chains
      The barriers holding her back
The rain beating drum stops
      And brings back what she lacked
Finally at peace
      She can let her breath go
Holding it in for so long
      The world could never know
The smile that disappeared
      Soon comes back to life
The child one so deathly feared
      Is finally alright
And as she let go
      She showed the world what she hid for so long
A beautiful child
      Who could never find home

TORRiLORRi
4/2/2007

# Rain Beat Drum

The day was dark
As the rain poured down
The streets were empty
Filled with silent sound

Deep beneath the surface
Of ~~~~ that smiling bright face
Locked away forever
Was the innocense that she chased

Dark & dreadful
The rain still beats
Inside of the soul
The one that weeps

Make the beating stop
Like a silenced drum
Make the sun come out
To show the world what it's hidden from

Uncover the mistery
That little girl sees
Because down in her soul
She starts to break free

She pulls from the chains
The barriers holding her back
The rain beating drum stops
And brings back what she lacked

Finally at peace
She can let her breath go
Holding it in for so long
The world could never know

The smile that disappeared
Soon comes back to life
The child one so deathly feared
Is finally alright

And as she let go
She showed the world what she hid for so long
A beautiful child
Who could never find home

By: Tori Hebert
1/2/07

# No One

As I turn the page
    Start a new story of my life
Hoping you'll exist
    And make the both of us alright
The tears continue to stain the page
    Your words continue to break my heart
Sometimes it just seems
    I can't stop from falling apart
I try so hard not to sin
    But the more you scream, the more it appeals
Should I take the blade to my wrists
    So there will be no more pain left to feel
I know you think it's talk
    But sometimes, I see no purpose for me
Sometimes I want to break down
    Let the blood set me free
This emotion's building up
    I grab for my Zoloft at night
I can't handle this pain
    I can't take this life
So as I scream
    And put this to where no one could read
At least this notebook knows
    That was the death of me

TORRiLORRi
5/24/2007

# No One

As I turn the page
Start a new story of my life
Hoping you'll exist
And make the both of us alright
The tears continue to stain the page
Your words continue to break my heart
Sometimes it just seems
I can't stop from falling apart
I try so hard not to sin
But the more you scream, the more it appeals
Should I take the blade to my wrists
So there will be no more pain left to feel
I know you think it's talk
But sometimes, I see no purpose for me
Sometimes I want to break down
Let the blood set me free
This emotions building up
I grab for my Zoloft at night
I can't handle this pain
I can't take this life
So as I scream
And put this to where no one could read
At least this notebook knows
That was the death of me

By: Torri Hobert
5/29/07

# Lost Lamb

I'm sick of being this way
      People looking at me in shock
Being a lost little lamb
      And being someone the world forgot
My words are too depressing
      My thoughts are too strong
The world thinks I'm a disgrace
      But they have all along
Will I end up a murderer
      Or an adult seeking revenge
Will I finally get some help
      Or will this demon come back again
I don't want to become crazy
      Or even grow to be this way
I don't want to have these issues
      Or hear what people have to say
It breaks my heart to look in a mirror
      To see what a devil I've become
This is not something I chose
      I just want it all to be gone

TORRiLORRi
5/25/2007

# Lost Lamb

I'm sick of being this way
People looking at me in shock
Being a lost little lamb
And being someone the world forgot
My words are too depressing
My thoughts are too strong
The world thinks I'm a disgrace
But they have all along
Will I end up a murderer
Or an adult seeking revenge
Will I finally get some help
Or will this demon come back again
I don't want to become crazy
Or even grow to be this way
I don't want to have these issues
Or hear what people have to say
It breaks my heart to look in a mirror
To see what a devil I've become
This is not something I chose
I just want it to all be gone

By: Tonni Rebout
8/25/07

# Acid Rain

I'm sitting here screaming
    Begging for an ear
For once, uncover your eyes
    And see my world from here
You say I'm doing well
    Without a smile on my face
I'd hate to see the bad
    Or the children of disgrace
I try to cover it up
    They said push it down inside
I try not to feel
    And finally just let my rules abide
The pounding becomes harder
    Is my heart in my throat?
The tears become stronger
    A sob held back, a silent choke
Think as you please
    But for once, may I please think?
Do as you want
    Without my heart put out on the brink
Ears sewn together
    Eyes taped shut
Remove the plastic from the surface
    See beneath the cut
It isn't a scab or wound
    Or a smile or laugh
Nothing is real in this world
    There's nothing you can take back
I try to push a grin
    Through the surface of the pain
I try not to show again
    As they said, "Just hide the rain
If it falls down
    There's nothing difficult to do
Just push the drops aside
    And finally be you"
But, words are the simplest invention
    They come and go as they please
Actions, on the other hand, can kill
    Go ahead, wear your heart on your sleeve
I want so bad to be healthy
    Be merely normal again
Care of only nothing
    And have the world be my friend

# Acid Rain

I'm just another normal face
    With a puncture and wounded soul
Maybe if I keep the emotions down
    Not another life will know
But it's hard to break through the rain
    The clouds continually block the sky
I can't work miracles and move mountains
    I'm only another life
My time is merely of the essence
    My heart beats increasing by the thought
Take this power away from my soul
    Take back the things the devil has brought
Don't let this heart break
    It seems to be made of glass
Everlasting fragile
    Another death with an open cask
I try not to let it hurt
    As I've said so many times before
Although I haven't let it show
    My heart has already hit the floor
I don't want to break
    Or let this tear be acid rain
I'm ready to give it my all
    Hand in hand we'll break away

TORRiLORRi
1/24/2008

# Acid Rain

I'm sitting here screaming
Begging for an ear
For once, uncover your eyes
And see my world from here
You say I'm doing well
Without a smile on my face
I'd hate to see the bad
Or the children of disgrace
I try to cover it up
They said push it down inside
I try not to feel
And finally just let my rulers abide
The pounding becomes harder
Is my heart in my throat?
The tears become stronger
A sob held back, a silent choke
Think as you please
But for once may I please think
Do as you want
Without my heart put out on the brink
Ears sewn together
Eyes taped shut
Remove the plastic from the surface
See beneath the cut

It isn't a scraper wound
Or a smile or laugh
Nothing is real in this world
There's nothing you can take back
I try to push the grin
Through the surface of the pain
I try not to show again
As they said "just hide the rain"
If it falls down
There's nothing difficult to do
Just push the drops aside
And finally be you.
But words are the simplest invention
They come & go as they please
Actions, on the other hand, can kill
Go ahead, wear your heart on your sleeve.
I want so bad to be healthy
Be merely normal again
Care of only nothing
And have the world be my friend
I'm just another normal face
With a puncture & wounded soul
Maybe if I keep the emotions down
Not another life will know

# Acid Rain

But it's hard to break through the rain
The clouds continually block the sky
I can't work miracles & move mountains
I'm only another life
My time is merely of the essence
My heart beats increasing by the thought
Take this power away from my soul
Take back the things the devil has brought
Don't let this heart break
It seems to be made of glass
Ever lasting fragile
Another death with an open cask
I try not to let it hurt
As I've said so many times before
Although I haven't let it show
My heart has already hit the floor.
I don't want to break
Or let this tear be acid rain
I'm ready to give it my all
Hand in hand we'll break away

By Torri Hebert
January 24, 08

# Our Own Fight
## Scene Setting

I'm 15 years old, my brother, Paul (JP/Butter), who is 10 years older than me has been my best friend all my life. He always understood me and never judged me for displaying my emotions. I was his Sweet Pea and he was my Butter. I looked up to him and, as with most younger siblings, wanted to be just like him when I grew up. My parents had divorced recently before this time, so Mom and I were trying to find our footing. JP was always there to help every step of the way.

Paul always felt the need to protect. The war and threat of danger to our country was heavy in 2008 with Saddam Hussein still at large. Paul, needing to do his part to protect our country, enlisted with the United States Army in the infantry division. Paul was in basic training in July of 2008 when this poem was written.

He had corresponded with my mother through letters in the mail. He wrote three letters to me as well. I didn't even want to read the letters when they arrived because I was so angry that he had left me all alone. It wasn't until his 3rd letter that I read them all and knew I had to respond. I've never been great at expressing my emotions through any way other than poetry. I knew to respond to him, it had to be a poem. I wrote this poem in my room in the early hours of the morning feeling every bit of anxiety from him being gone. This poem is all I mailed him. I didn't feel as if anything else needed to be said.

JP still says to this day how when he received my poem it was like the last verse of the song "Letters From Home" by John Michael Montgomery. Summing up the verse the soldier's father tells him how his son has made him proud. It follows up with the final chorus saying how he reads the letter to his training buddies, but no one laughs because there is nothing funny about a soldier crying and how he wipes his eyes, puts the letter in his pocket, and gets back to work.

Paul no longer had the original poem for me to scan into my book. It didn't matter though because I have this poem embedded in my soul. Many nights I would put myself to sleep by repeating this poem in my head over and over. I hope you enjoy seeing the raw relationship between baby sister and big brother.

# Our Own Fight

He stands and fights his battle
    As I crouch and fight mine
He protects the entire world
    When I can't even defeat my mind
He's always pushed to help others
    Because it distracts him from himself
But I see the hero within
    Within the man I know like no one else
I've been fighting my mind tonight
    Debating on how I feel
Missing every second I had with you
    Assuming this isn't real
You see, I've been fighting this demon lately
    But not letting it show through
Because the truth is I'd rather you here, not doing your dream
    But instead, I'm missing you
You'll have the front row to history
    But who said I wanted MY everything that close?
Near danger, & terror, & enemies
    Near everything you chose
I'm proud of you beyond belief
    But it's hard sitting up these nights
Knowing your training for what could be the end
    Knowing it could be the end of your life-long fight
I've been thinking a lot lately
    More than my mere mind racing scheme
I never thought I'd be scared to see you happy
    But by happy, I never knew this would be what you'd mean
JP, I'm scared to death right now
    Cliché, but shaking in my boots
You should know I'm worried, no, terrified
    All because I love YOU
Don't leave me in this world
    You know I can't handle it myself
Besides you just can't
    Because you make me laugh like no one else
It's 5 am and I haven't come to reason
    I can't abandon what could happen to you
You're all I have left, Butter
    You're all I look up to
I'm sorry it took so long to respond
    But I couldn't bring myself to write
And now I'm calling out, screaming into thin air
    For you to return tonight

# Our Own Fight

It isn't that I want you to be unhappy
      But why couldn't you be happy somewhere safe?
But, safe doesn't run through our blood
      We're always on the edge of escape
Well you've escaped this
      But I still sit up every night
Wondering why you'd escape me
      I guess we never saw the light
So now,
      Sitting in the breeze
Staring to nothing
      I slip to my knees
Pray for your love
      Pray for your life
Pray for your battle
      But even more for your fight
So when you remember home
      Remember me even more
Because I'm fighting a battle as well
      That's killing at the core
Hold my heart within your own
      And kiss the stars tonight
Because I'm staring up with you
      Defeating the sister of a soldier's fight.

TORRiLORRi
7/18/2008
Dedicated to Paul Matt (JP/Butter)

# The World's Darkest Day

The dawn falls to dusk
    As the sun fades to grey
The sky hits the ground
    On the world's darkest day

The stars will burn out
    The laughter will hide
The tears will fall to the floor
    While the smiles subside

The wind won't blow at all
    As the world has reached its end
Goodbye to you world
    Goodbye to you, dear friend

As my tears stain these words
    And my face falls to a frown
Please awake me from this nightmare
    Awake me before I drown

Has the world fallen asleep?
    Or drifted into oblivion too?
I will never know another soul
    As radiant as you

The leaves fall to ashes
    The sun will never stay
A heartbeat is lost
    On the world's darkest day

TORRiLORRi
4/1/2009
Dedicated to John Nathan Carmena

# Hymn Icarus

Under the stars
    I look up to the sky
And I recall all the moments
    You helped me fly
The battle was fought
    And finally won
A peak through the clouds
    Comes a ray of the sun
On the darkest nights
    With little sleep
You're the one
    That reaches out to me
The wind blows
    And the trees shift
I never knew
    That this would be it
Hold me now
    As we hold forever dear
I'll never release this
    It's becoming so clear
The clouds drift
    And the sun is now shining through
I've found myself
    Because of you

TORRiLORRi
5/4/2009

# Hymn Icarus

Under the stars
I look up to the sky
And I recall all the moments
You helped me fly
The battle was fought
And finally won
A peak through the clouds
Comes a ray of the sun
On the darkest nights
With little sleep
You're the one
That reaches out to me
The wind blows
And the trees shift
I never knew
That this would be it
Hold me now
As we hold forever dear
I'll never release this
It is becoming so clear
The clouds drift
And the sun is now shining through
I've found myself,
Because of you

Terri Hebert
5/9/09

# Punctured Puppeteer

Play with my heart
        To you it's only a game
Crush my soul
        And make me change
Destroy my life
        With the flip of your wrist
I'm your puppet after all
        I do as you insist
You're controlling my life
        Controlling the person I don't want to be
Will I ever be my own
        Will my soul ever be free
Is it too much
        To live my own life
Because living by your rules
        Has only brought me strife
I'm cutting the strings on my arms and feet
        Once and for all
From now on I'm on my own
        And I'm ready for this fall

                                        TORRiLORRi
                                        2009ish

# Punctured Puppeteer

Play with my heart
To you it's only a game
Crush my soul
And make me change
Destroy my life
With the flip of your wrist
I'm your puppet after all
I do as you insist
~~scribbled out~~
~~scribbled out~~
You're controlling my life
Controlling the person I don't want to be
Will I ever be my own
Will my soul ever be free
Is it too much
To live my own life
Because living by your rules
Has only brought me strife
I'm cutting the strings on my arms & feet
Once & for all
From now on I'm on my own
And I'm ready for this fall.

By Torri Orr 2009ish

# Chaos Before The Calm

Just when you think the world's gone crazy
    And the chaos has become insane
Take a step back from it all
    And find shelter from the rain
Because after the storm is over
    The calm is guaranteed
You must first experience the worst
    Before the wretched weather decides to cease
In this life we must conquer the storm
    So please take me by the palm
Two is always better than one
    And there will always be chaos before the calm

TORRiLORRi
4/1/2011

# Chaos Before The Calm

Just when you think the world's gone crazy
And the chaos has become insane
Take a step back from it all
And find shelter from the rain
Because after the storm is over
The calm is garenteed
You must experience the worst
Before the wretched weather decides to cease
In this life we must consider the storm
So please take me by the palm
Two is always better than one
And there will always be chaos before the calm

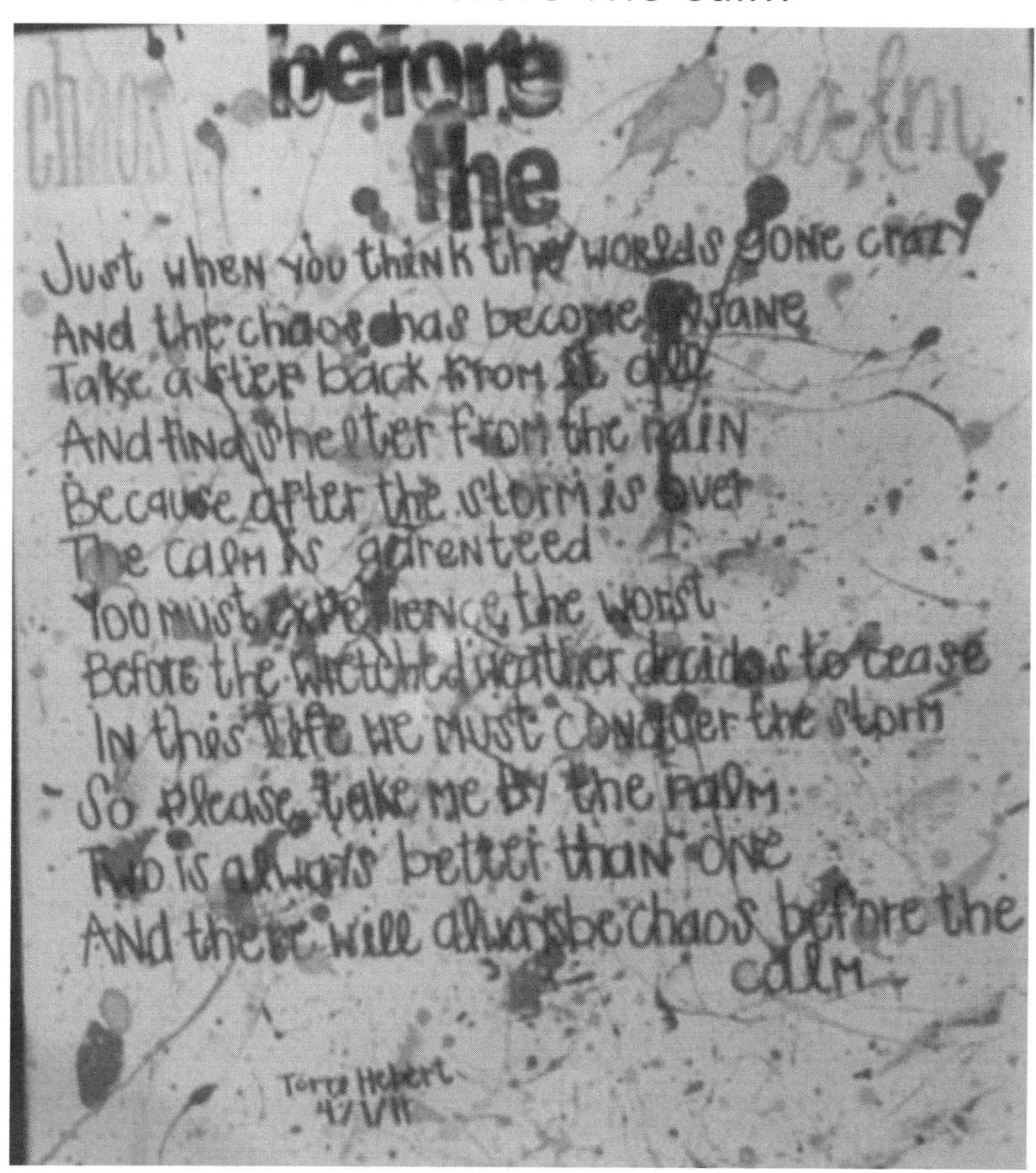

Torri Hebert

# Henri

Listen to Momma, Henri
        Take my word to heart
This is Momma's life lessons for you
        So let's begin from the start
Hold on to your childhood, my love
        For as long as you can
Cherish your youth and innocence
        Do you understand?
Begin every day with a prayer to the Lord
        Thanking him for the adventures He's placed in front of you
Never let the thoughts of yesterday plague your mind
        Commence each day anew
Realize that a storm can't last forever
        And once the rain runs out
The beauty of a rainbow will be waiting to greet you
        Peeking through the clouds
End your days talking with God
        Praising Him for your journey of the day
Even if you think you've reached a dead end
        Pay close attention and He will show you what he needs to say
Take each day as a blessing
        Rejoice for time spent with family and friends
Because in all reality, my dear
        The Lord could have a much bigger plan for them
Never regret the mistakes you've made
        Simply learn from them and move on
Because, sometimes through mistakes are brought miracles
        That is how I received you, my precious son
Laugh at your enemy's hatred
        And smile at their glares
Hold on to the ones you love
        And always show just how much you care
Respect your elders my sunshine
        Yes ma'am and no sir are something I expect
Never allow someone to speak down to you
        Make sure those you care for, you protect
True happiness exists within your own heart
        The only one you can count on is yourself
Loss is a part of this life
        Never allow a faulty friend cause you to dwell
Wish upon a star
        And dream your biggest dreams
With heart and determination
        You can accomplish anything

# Henri

Make pictures in the clouds
    And at 11:11 make a wish
Know that you're Momma's heart and soul
    And absolutely no love could be greater than this
Ponder your favorite memories often
    Always keep them fresh in your mind
Hold on to forever
    And love like crazy, to the end of time

TORRiLORRi
11/6/2012
Dedicated to The Best Henri Ever<3
(Pronounced Henry)

# Henri

Listen to Momma, Henri
Take my word to heart
This is Momma's life lessons for you
So let's begin from the start
Hold on to your childhood, my love
For as long as you can
Cherish your youth & innocence
Do you understand?
Begin every day with a prayer to the Lord
Thanking him for the adventures he's placed in front of you
Never let the thoughts of yesterday plague your mind
Commence each day anew
Realize that a storm can't last forever
And once the rain runs out
The beauty of a rainbow will be waiting to greet you
Peeking through the clouds
End your days talking with God
Praising him for your journey of the day
Even if you think you've reached a dead end
Pay close attention and he will show you what he needs to say
Take each day as a blessing
Rejoice for time spent with family and friends
Because in all reality, my dear
The Lord could have a much bigger plan for them

# Henri

Never regret the mistakes you've made
Simply learn from them & move on
Because, sometimes through mistakes are brought miracles
That is how I received you, my precious son
Laugh at your enemy's hatred
And smile at their glares
Hold on to the ones you love
And always show just how much you care
Respect your elders my sunshine
Yes ma'am & no sir are something I expect
Never allow someone to speak down to you
Make sure those you care for, you protect
True happiness exists within your own heart
The only one you can count on is yourself
Loss is apart of this life
Never allow a faulty friend cause you to dwell
Wish upon a star
And dream your biggest dreams
With heart and determination
You can accomplish anything
Make pictures in the clouds
And at 11:11 make a wish
Know that your momma's heart & soul
And absolutely no love could be greater than this
Ponder your favorite memories often
Always keep them fresh in your mind
Hold on to forever
And love like crazy, to the end of time

By Torri Hebert
11/6/12

For Henri Donald Hebert. My dearest son. Momma loves you to the moon & back ♡

# Soundless Scream

A whisper in the wind
    Or a mere echo from the past?
A shadow through the darkness
    Or your mind expelling its wrath?
A coolness in the breeze
    That's never been noticed before
Lie down on the grass
    As you feel the shiver from its core
You call out for help
    No one can save you now
Holding on for dear life
    As you sink into the ground
Searching for an end
    When the beginning is left unknown
Wander through infinity
    Looking for your home
A chill in the dusk
    That becomes masked by the dawn
The search can't continue forever
    Because your time is nearly gone

TORRiLORRi
6/7/2012

# Soundless Scream

Soundless Scream
A whisper in the wind
Or a mere echo from the past?
A shadow through the darkness
Or your mind expelling its wrath?
A coolness in the breeze
That's never been noticed before
Lie down on the grass
As you feel the shiver from its core
You call out for help
No one can save you now
Holding on for dear life
As you sink into the ground
Searching for an end
When the beginning is left unknown
Wander through infinity
Looking for your home
A chill in the dusk
That becomes masked by the dawn
The search can't continue forever
Because your time is nearly gone

JS 6/7/12

# Grand Plans

I felt as if I came so far
    And simply threw it down the drain
Maybe I'm over-reacting
    Surely sunshine will follow this rain
I know I'm the one at fault
    Henri, I'm so sorry I've let you down
Momma promises I will fix this
    And turn all of this around
I thought I had my life together
    But maybe I was wrong
Straighten up your act, Victoria
    Before all you've worked for is gone
It's time to grow up now
    For God's sake leave your childhood behind
Let go of your pain, your hurt, your anger
    After 12 years it's time to clear it from your mind
You'll never survive adulthood
    If you don't suppress the past
Stop reflecting on how things should have been
    Because this life passes much too fast
"Life passes most people by while they're making grand plans for it"
    I don't want this life to pass me by
I will break through this barrier
    This is my time to shine

                TORRiLORRi
                1/15/2013

# Grand Plans

By: Torri Lorri
01/15/2013

## Grand Plans

I felt as if I came so far
And simply threw it down the drain
Maybe I'm over-reacting
Surely sunshine will follow this rain
I know I'm the one at fault
Henri, I'm so sorry I've let you down
Momma promises I will fix this
And turn all of this around
I thought I had my life together
But maybe I was wrong
Straighten up your act, Victoria
Before all you've worked for is gone
It's time to grow up now
For God's sake leave your childhood behind
Let go of your pain, your hurt, your anger
After 12 years its time to clear'd from your mind
You'll never survive adulthood
If you don't supress the past
Stop reflecting on how things should have been
B/c this life passes much to fast.
"Life passes most people by while
       they're making grand plans for it"
I don't want this life to pass me by
I will break through this barrier
This is my time to shine.

# Evan

As the breeze rolls in
    With the clouds overhead
And the rain sinks down
    To your final bed
I try to look above
    For an answer in the sky
But as I watch it fall
    I lose my sense of mind
The ground begins to tremble
    As my heart breaks a little more
Because I know it's time to say goodbye
    While you're knocking on Heaven's door
Why does the world seem to end
    As we lay you down to rest
I wish I could hug you one last time
    Or see your smile at best
But, when you lay beneath the Earth
    And the stillness comes about
A peace settles in my soul
    Because I know you've found water through the drought

TORRiLORRi
9/16/2014
Dedicated to Evan Glenn Schittone

# Evan

## Evan

As the breeze rolls in
With the clouds overhead
And the rain sinks down
To your final bed
I try to look above
For an answer in the sky
But as I watch it fall
I lose my sense of mind
The ground begins to tremble
As my heart breaks a little more
Because I know it's time to say goodbye
While you're knocking on Heaven's door
Why does the world seem to end
As we lay you down to rest
I wish I could hug you one last time
Or see your smile at best
But, when you lay beneath the Earth
And the stillness comes about
A peace settles in my soul
Because I know you've found water through the drought

Terri Hebert
9/16/14

Written for Evan Schittone
R.I.P. sweet friend ♡

# 24 Years Old

The nip of the breeze
      The emptiness in the air
Didn't seem so strong
      When you were there
February is here
      Tomorrow's the day
24 years
      And nothing to say
It's nearly been 5 months
      Since we've laid you down
It's hard to believe
      You're six feet in the ground
I feel so selfish
      Wishing you were here
To soothe my aching heart
      And dry my falling tears
I know you're at peace
      And your life-long battle is done
But I'm stuck here, without you
      And mine has just begun
Sometimes, I swear you're here
      Watching me break in two
How could this be,
      A life without you?
I miss you so much Evan
      It hurts to the core
I wish I could have helped you
      But I tried endless times before
Fly high now baby boy
      I swear I'll be ok
We'll meet again eventually
      Someday, at heaven's gates

TORRiLORRi
2/6/2015
Dedicated to Evan Glenn Schittone

# 24 Years Old

I miss you so much Evan
It hurts to the core
I wish I could have helped you
But I tried endless times before
Fly high now baby boy
I swear I'll be ok
We'll meet again eventually
Someday, at heavens gates

2/6/2015

Dedicated to Evan Glenn Schittone

# In-Between

As the sun beams down
    With the rustling of the leaves
You feel the wind all around
    As it whispers through the trees
Where are we headed
    In this big game of life?
Will the answers come
    While we rest our head upon our pillows tonight?
Do we dream of the future
    Hoping for all it may hold?
Turning our face to the sun
    And our backs from the cold
Reaching for the stars
    Leaping for the moon
Because the sad truth is
    It will end too soon
Striving for perfection
    However, with mistakes along the way
Molding the person we're meant to be
    The one we will embrace
As I close my eyes
    And drift off once more
I'll reach for the unopened portal
    No matter of the fear I had before
I'll never learn what's possible
    If I don't ever take this chance
I may discover my reality
    Or forever be lost in a trance
Either way it goes
    I'd be crazy if I didn't try
Finding the "in-between" non-fiction and fantasy
    Is something most of us look by
Whatever it may be
    Sleeping or awake
A dream is a dream
    A risk I'm willing to take

TORRiLORRi
7/8/2015

# In-Between

As the sun beams down
With the rustling of the leaves
You feel the wind all around
As it whispers through the trees
Where are we headed
In this big game of life?
Will the answers come
While we rest our head upon our pillows tonight?
Do we dream of the future,
Hoping for all it may hold?
Turning our face to the sun
And our backs from the cold.
Reaching for the stars
Leaping for the moon
Because the sad truth is
It will end too soon
Striving for perfection
However with mistakes along the way
Molding the person we're meant to be
The one we will embrace
As I close my eyes
And drift off once more
I'll reach for the unopened portal
No matter of the fear I had before
I'll never learn what's possible
If I don't ever take this chance.
I may discover my reality
Or forever be lost in a trance
Either way it goes
I'd be crazy if I didn't try
Finding the "in-between" nonfiction & fantasy
Is something most of us look by
Whatever it may be
Sleeping or awake
A dream is a dream
A risk I'm willing to take

Terri Hebert
7/8/15

# Silent Serenade

Am I really here right now
      Lying in your bed?
Is this a dream? A fantasy?
      I'd rather dream instead
I can feel your touch
      When early morning sets in
I can hear your voice
      Feel your whispers on my skin
I open my eyes
      To find yours, right there looking down
I smile at the thought
      That neither one of us has to make a sound
We just are, here together
      We simply exist
Words mustn't feel the silence
      We'd rather fill it with a kiss
I've been yearning for you
      Late at night, hundreds of miles away
Now that I'm here, breathing you in
      I'm at a loss for words to say
But words no longer matter
      When I see that look in your eyes
You whisper in my ear, "Baby, I'm here"
      And all of a sudden, you've frozen time

TORRiLORRi
7/16/2015

# Silent Serenade

Am I really here right now
lying in your bed?
Is this a dream? A fantasy?
I'd rather dream instead
I can feel your touch
when early morning sets in
I can hear your voice
Feel your whispers on my skin
I open my eyes
To find yours right there looking down
I smile at the thought
That neither one of us has to make a sound
We just are, here together
We simply exist
Words mustn't feel the silence
We'd rather fill it with a kiss
I've been yearning for you
Late at night, hundreds of miles away
Now that I'm here, breathing you in
I'm at a loss for words to say
But words no longer matter
When I see that look in your eyes
You whisper in my ear, "Baby I'm here"
And all of a sudden you've frozen time

Torri Hebert
7/16/15

# Meet You There

As I lay here in this bed
    Awaiting my dreams at night
I pray I'll see you there
    So I know you're still at my side
A year has passed today
    Since you've gone home
And every moment of every day
    I remember the love you've shown
I've felt you in my weakest moments
    Noticed all of the signs you leave
Heard you say, "It'll be alright"
    When I'm nearly too broken to breathe
You're here with me in my happiest days
    Rejoicing with me in cheers
Holding my hand through the most difficult of all
    Through all of my deepest fears
I'll meet you in the night
    While not a soul makes a sound
As we stand still in time
    And the clock spins around and around
I'll meet you in my dreams
    For death can't part us there
I'll meet you in my dreams
    Where all is true, all is right, all is fair

TORRiLORRi
9/16/2015
Dedicated to Evan Glenn Schittone

# Meet You There

As I lay here in this bed
Awaiting my dreams at night
I pray I'll see you there
So I know you're still at my side
A year has passed today
Since you've gone home
And every moment of every day
I remember the love you've shown
I've felt you in my weakest moments
Noticed all of the signs you leave
Heard you say, "It'll be alright"
When I'm nearly too broken to breathe
You're here with me in my happiest days
Rejoicing with me in cheers
Holding my hand through the most difficult of all
Through all of my deepest fears
I'll meet you in the night
While not a soul makes a sound
~~I'll meet you in my dreams~~ As we stand still
~~And~~ the clock spins around & around in time
I'll meet you in my dreams
For death can't part us there
I'll meet you in my dream
Where all is true, all is right, all is fair

9/16/15
Torri Hebert
Written for Evan Schittone RIP my love

**LIVE the life you LOVE**

# Chorus Of Angels

The angels begin to sing
    As you've finally made it home
Eternity with our Creator
    Such a beautiful song
I look up to the heavens
    And rejoice for your time spent here
God lent such a beautiful angel
    That always held love so dear
He knew what He was doing
    When He put you on this earth
To honor and protect your family
    For whatever it is worth
I remember being a child
    Chasing the dog in your backyard
Running straight into your clothesline
    And falling down so hard
You picked me up, brushed me off
    Said, "Honey, you'll be alright
The pain will go away shortly."
    But I'll have that memory, all of my life
God couldn't have chosen a better soul
    To joyfully rise up and sing
With the chorus of His angels
    Who guard and protect the hearts they've seen

        TORRiLORRi
        11/10/2015
    Dedicated to Mildred New (Mammaw)

# Chorus Of Angels

The angels begin to sing
As you've finally made it home
Eternity with our Creator
Such a beautiful song
~~Something through this life~~
I look up to the heavens
And rejoice for your time spent here
God lent such a beautiful angel
That always held love so dear
He knew what He was doing
When He put you on this earth
To honor and protect your family
For whatever it is worth
I remember being a child
Chasing the dog in your back yard
Running straight into your clothes line
And falling down so hard
You picked me up, brushed me off
Said, "Honey, you'll be alright.
The pain will go away shortly."
But I'll have that memory all of my life.
God couldn't have chosen a better soul
To joyfully rise up & sing
With the chorus of His angels
Who guard & protect the hearts they've seen

Dedicated to: Terri Lorri
Mildred New 11/10/2015
(Mammaw)

# All You See

Sometimes I wonder
      What all you see
When you hug my waist
      And smile up at me
I try so hard to be steady
      And hold my head up high
Teach you how to be strong
      Even more, how to survive
This road isn't easy
      But we do the best we can
I try my damnedest to show you
      How to be a man

          TORRiLORRi
          2016ish

# All You See

Sometimes I wonder
What all you see
When you hug my waist
And smile up at me
I try so hard to be steady
And hold my head up high
Teach you how to be strong
Even more, how to survive
This road isn't easy
But we do the best we can
I try my ~~best~~ damnedest to show you
How to be a man

JS 2016 ish

# Self-Created

Here I am again
        15 years old
No more fight left in me
        But a war within my soul
Will I ever break free
        Will I ever be ok
In the grips of anxiety
        With nothing more to say
"Why is she acting crazy?"
        "Why can't she control herself?"
But will you ever understand
        This self-created hell
I thought this war was over
        The pain within my heart
This dark passenger
        That's been present from the start
I bottle it all up
        Try to fight the best I can
But sometimes I can't stop it
        Sometimes I can hardly stand
Trying to breathe
        Gasping for air
With a weight on my chest
        I can no longer bare
When will I escape
        When will the struggle be done
But I'm fighting a battle
        That can never be won

TORRiLORRi
4/28/2016

# Self-Created

Here I am again
15 years old
No more fight left in me
But a war within my soul
Will I ever break free
Will I ever be ok
In the grips of anxiety
With nothing more to say
"Why is she acting crazy?"
"Why can't she control herself?"
But will you ever understand
This self-created hell
I thought this was over
The pain within my heart
This dark passenger
That's been present from the start
I bottle it all up
Try to fight the best I can
But sometimes I can't stop it
Sometimes I can hardly stand
Trying to breathe
Gasping for air
With a weight on my chest
I can no longer bare
When will I escape
When will the struggle be done
But I'm fighting a fight
That can never be won.

4/20/16

# Angels Dwell

While the wind starts to whistle
    And the trees begin to weep
I'll lie on the cool grass
    And drift off into sleep
Remembering a place
    Where the sky is the brightest blue
Remembering a day
    When I first learned of you
It all made so much sense
    Why I felt so alone
A piece of me was missing
    A part of me was gone
I found you, and lost you
    All at the same time
My heart rose and plummeted
    Confronting death in disguise
How can a child understand death
    When I don't even understand myself
Or know you are safe with God
    Where all the other angels dwell

TORRiLORRi
5/14/2016
Dedicated to Whitney Nicole Hebert (Nikki)

# Angels Dwell

While the wind starts to whistle
And the trees begin to weep
I'll lie on the cool grass
And drift off into sleep
Remembering a place
Where the sky is the brightest blue
Remembering a day
When I first learned of you
It all made so much sense
Why I felt so alone
A piece of me was missing
A part of me was gone
I found you, and lost you
All at the same time
My heart rose & plumeted
Confronting death in disguise
How can a child understand death
When I don't even understand myself
Or know you are safe with God
Where all the other angels dwell

5/19/16

# Hue Of Blue

Though the moon is full and the stars are bright
      The darkness continues to grow
Creeping into the soul and heart
      Overpowering everything you know
Will the birds cease to sing
      Will the clouds halt their dance
Or the willows ever whisper
      Proposing another chance
Your heart won't continue to beat
      If you don't will it to
You mustn't simply trudge through life
      Because the sky's lost its hue of blue
The world will continue to spin
      Whether you're here or not
So make the most of what you have
      And do the best with what you've got

TORRiLORRi
5/14/2016

# Hue Of Blue

Though the moon is full & the stars are bright
The darkness continues to grow
Creeping into the soul and the heart
Overpowering everything you know
Will the birds cease to sing
Will the clouds halt their dance
Or the willows ever whisper
Proposing another chance
Your heart won't continue to beat
If you don't will it to
You mustn't simply trudge through life
Because the sky's lost its hue of blue
The world will continue to spin
Whether you're here or not
So make the most of what you have
And do the best with what you've got

Torri Hebert
5/14/16

# Short Season

The days continue to pass
      As the pain begins to ease
I've held on for so long
      But it's time to set you free
This life is an adventure,
      People pass through at certain times
Maybe your time is gone
      And I should say goodbye
I'm ready to turn the page
      And allow a new chapter to begin
Let go of all the pain
      And give myself room to mend
Pain is a part of this life
      Heartbreaks are too
Maybe you were just a lesson to me
      But now it's time to be through
I appreciate you being in my life
      For the split second you were here
You taught me to be myself
      And never back down from my fears
Your time is gone now
      It's time we begin anew
But I'll never forget
      Even if our moments were few
Great adventures lie ahead of me
      Simple memories lie behind
Even if given the chance
      I would never press rewind
Obstacles are placed before us
      So we may grow and learn
Look out world
      I'm ready for my turn

TORRiLORRi
2018-2019

# Short Season

The days continue to pass
As the pain begins to ease
I've held on for so long
But it's time to set you free
This life is an adventure,
People pass through at certain times
Maybe your time is gone
And I should say goodbye
I'm ready to turn the page
And allow a new chapter to begin
Let go of all the pain
And give myself room to mend
Pain is a part of this life
Heartbreaks are too
Maybe you were simply a lesson for me
But now it's time to be through.
I appreciate you being in my life
For the split second you were here
You taught me to be myself
And never back down from my fears
Your time is gone now
It's time we begin anew
But I'll never forget
Even if our moments were few
Great adventures lie ahead of me
Simple memories lie behind
Even if given the chance
I would never press rewind
Obstacles are placed before us
So we may grow & learn
Look out world
I'm ready for my turn

TORRI LOKKI 2018 - 2019

# Magnificent Red Marble

A weekend trip to Texas
    For Mawmaw's birthday
It's a 10-hour journey
    Just going one way
Arrive Saturday morning
    Right after 3 AM
Party all night Saturday
    Then pack up Sunday to leave again
As my son and I drove away
    A sadness crept up
"Our fun had just begun"
    "That couldn't be enough"
We embark on the road
    And the sun begins to fade
The moon peaks out
    Ready for its chance to play
The moon was different tonight though
    Huge and bright and crisp
I asked Henri if he noticed a change
    He said, "Mom, it's probably just the eclipse."
We drive on a little further
    With the moon straight ahead
Once the eclipse has begun
    The moon took a hue of red
We pulled over
    In a "no-name" town
Admiring the beauty
    God had sent down
It was a brisk night though
    We quickly got back in the car
Set back on the road
    Praying the moon would follow that far
Set the cruise control
    Open up the moon-roof
Gaze at His painting
    And wonder how anyone could need proof
I have a lot of demons
    Struggling inside of me
But my Savior, my Lord, my God
    Still gave me a front row seat
The night was clear
    Not a cloud in sight
Going through Jennings
    I could see every star in the sky

# Magnificent Red Marble

Once we got to Crowley
    The blood moon was at its peek
It looked like a magnificent red marble
    Leaving me unable to speak
I try to breathe it in
    Hold on to it for as long as I can
File it in my memories
    So I can recall God's plan
No moment lasts forever
    They all must come to an end
But hold on to the best times
    So hopefully they come around again
I was mesmerized by the night
    All the stars fell into place
Dancing around the moon
    Emphasizing all of God's Grace
Once I witnessed this magic
    A peace washed over my soul
"God is giving you an opportunity, Torri
    Get out there and go!"

                TORRiLORRi
                1/23/2019

# Magnificent Red Marble

A weekend trip to Texas
For Mawmaws birthday
Its a 10 hour journey
Just going one way
Arrive Saturday morning
Right after 3 AM
Party all night Saturday
Then pack up Sunday to leave again
As my son & I drove away
A sadness crept up
"Our fun had just begun"
"That couldn't be enough"
We embark on the road
And the sun begins to fade
The moon peaks out
Ready for us chance to play
The moon was different tonight though
Huge, & bright, & crisp
I asked Henri if he noticed a change
He said, "Mom its probably just the eclipse."
We drive on a little further
With the moon straight ahead
Once the eclipse began
The moon took a hue of red
We pulled over
In a "No-Name" town
Admiring the beauty
God had sent down
It was a brisk night though
So we quickly got back in the car
Set back on the road
Praying the moon would follow that far

# Magnificent Red Marble

Set the cruise control
Open up the moon-roof
Gaze at His painting
And wonder how anyone could need proof
I have a lot of demons
Struggling inside of me
But my Savior, my Lord, my God
Still gave me a front row seat
The night was clear
Not a cloud in sight
Going through Jennings
I could see every star in the sky
Once we got to Crowley
The blood moon was at its peak
It looked like a magnificent red marble
Leaving me unable to speak
I try to breathe it in
Hold on to it for as long as I can
File it in my memories
So I can recall God's plan
No moment lasts forever
They all must come to an end
But hold on to the best times
So hopefully they come around again
I was mesmerized by the night
All the stars fell into place
Dancing around the moon
Emphasizing all of God's Grace
Once I witnessed this magic
A peace washed over my soul
"God is giving you an opportunity, Torri
Get out there, & go!"

Torri Hebert
1/23/19

# Temperant

I've been on this dark and lonely road
    For most of my life
Where only shadows grow
    Causing fear and strife
Never seeing the potential
    Never noticing the light
That you saw immediately
    And claimed shown so bright
I don't know what you've done to me, boy
    I don't know how you made me see
All the happiness within my soul
    That I've kept behind lock and key
The sky's a little brighter
    As the sun kisses my skin
Reminding me that finally
    I can love myself again
My perception has changed
    The world isn't always so dark
Behind every life is a purpose
    And mine has become a work of art
You gave me that gift
    The greatest gift of all
The courage to stand in the eye of the storm
    And know with certainty, "I will not fall"
Thank you for everything you've done
    Thank you for all you've helped me see
From the bottom of my soul to the top of my heart
    Love forever, the thankful me

TORRiLORRi
2/4/2019

# Temperant

Temperant
I've been on this dark & lonely road
For most of my life
Where only shadows grow
Causing fear & strife
Never seeing the potential
Never noticing the light
That you saw immediately
And claimed shown so bright
I don't know what you've done to me, boy
I don't know how you made me see
All the happiness within my soul
That I've kept behind lock & key
The sky's a little brighter
As the sun kisses my skin
Reminding me that finally
I can love myself again
My perception has changed
The world isn't always so dark
Behind every life is a purpose
And mine has become a work of art
You gave me that gift
The greatest gift of all
The courage to stand in the eye of the storm
And know with certainty, "I will not fall"
Thank you for everything you've done
Thank you for all you've helped me see
From the bottom of my soul to the top of my heart
Love forever, the thankful me ♡
   Torri Hebert
   2/4/19

# Henri's Heightening

You have grown so much
    From the baby you used to be
You impress me more every day
    With your wit, humor, and empathy
You're becoming such a man
    At only 7 years old
You are so aware of your manners
    And mostly do as you're told
The other day as we were leaving Walmart
    You walked closest to the street
Told me about how you're the man of the house
    And it was your duty to protect me
While cooking dinner tonight
    You wandered in, asking to help
Started stirring the potatoes
    As you whispered, "You don't have to do it all by yourself."
And my heart burst with pride
    At the fact that you are so aware
So conscientious of others emotions
    And always offering to be there
A man in the making
    Happening right before my eyes
I love the gentleman you're becoming
    But I wish we could slow down time

TORRiLORRi
2/15/2019

# Henri's Heightening

You have grown so much
From the baby you used to be
You impress me more every day
With your wit, humor, & empathy
You're becoming such a man
At only 7 years old
You are so aware of your manners
And mostly do as you're told
The other day as we were leaving Walmart
You walked closest to the street
Told me about how you're the man of the house
And it was your duty to protect me
While cooking dinner tonight
You wandered in, asking to help
Started stirring the potatoes
As you whispered, "you don't have to do it all by yourself"
And my heart burst with pride
At the fact that you are so awake
So conscientious of others emotions
And always offering to be there
A man in the making
Happening right before my eyes
I love the gentleman you're becoming
But I wish we could slow down time

Torri Hebert 2/15/19

# Mimic

The time keeps passing
    And the world continues to spin
I feel like it's finally under control
    But it all comes crashing in again
I want to control my anxiety
    I want to remain calm
Before I can even grasp it
    I'm shaking at the palms
My chest gets tight
    Extend my neck, choke for air
As my ears start ringing
    My knees give out from there
My head is throbbing
    Mimicking the race of my heart
I've been told, "It's only in your head."
    But it's been this way from the start
Anxiety is debilitating
    The attacks are even worse
I pray that no one
    Ever has to endure this wretched curse
Most days are better
    But some days are tough
Nonetheless I'll trudge on
    Until my composure is enough

TORRiLORRi
2/15/2019

# Mimic

Mimic

The time keeps passing
And the world continues to spin
I feel like it's finally under control
But it all comes crashing in again
I want to control my anxiety
I want to remain calm
Before I can even grasp it
I'm shaking at the palms
My chest gets tight
Extend my neck, choke for air
As my ears start ringing
My knees give out from there
My head is throbbing
Mimicking the race of my heart
I've been told, "It's only in your head"
But it's been this way from the start
Anxiety is debilitating
The attacks are even worse
I pray that no one
Ever has to endure this wretched curse
Most days are better
But some days are tough
Nonetheless I'll trudge on
Until my composure is enough

    Torri Hebert 2/15/19

# Starboard Soul

From the darkest of nights
    To the brightest of days
From the shattering of glass
    To Seeing the soul that you saved
Past moments of doubt
    Through overwhelming fear
Constantly praying
    You'll always be here
I know it can't be simple
    Taming the tormented sea
But somehow you held the course
    And found your way to me
Providing me your anchor
    Your stability through the storm
Healing all that's broken
    Mending all that's torn
You saved me from the jagged sea
    The wretched rain, the rushing waves
You are the calm my soul always sought
    My hallelujah, my saving grace

TORRiLORRi
9/7/2019

# Starboard Soul

From the darkest of nights
To the brightest of days
From the shattering of glass
To seeing the soul that you saved
Past moments of doubt
Through overwhelming fear
Constantly praying
You'll always be here
I know it can't be simple
Taming the tormented sea
But somehow you held the course
And found your way to me
Providing me your anchor
Your stability through the storm
Healing all that's broken
Mending all that's torn
You saved me from the jagged sea
The wrechet rain, the rushing waves
You are the calm my soul always seeked
My hallelujah, my saving grace

Torri Hebert
9/7/19

# Torri's Story

So much time has passed
      I was certain the desire had left
Yet here I am again
      Desperately grasping for my safety net
I thought I had it all figured out
      Positive I knew the true Torri
And then, emotional distress arrives
      Holding my hand, coaxing me back to the same old story
I know it's wrong, a silent cry for help
      But when my life is out of control, I crave the release
I crave the control, the decision, the power
      And the endorphins that put my body at ease
This has always been dealt with
      The depression, the anxiety
Yet, according to a recent diagnosis
      There's a bipolar side of me
Does that explain the elated feeling, manic episodes
      Often experiencing cloud nine
Only to come crashing down
      Landing in this deep, dark, depressive state of mind
Will I ever pull myself from the depths
      Hold my heart at even keel
Or am I doomed to this constant tug-of-war
      Never once knowing which side is real

TORRiLORRi
3/26/2020

# Torri's Story

Torri's Story
So much time has passed
I was certain the desire had left
Yet here I am again
Desperately grasping for my safety net
I thought I had it all figured out
Positive I knew the true Torri
And then, emotional distress arrives
Holding my hand, coaxing me back to the same old story
I know it's wrong, a silent cry for help
But when my life is out of control, I crave the release
I crave the control, the decision, the power
And the endorphins that put my body at ease
This has always been dealt with
The depression, the anxiety
Yet, according to a recent diagnosis
There's a bipolar side of me
Does that explain the elated feeling, manic episodes
Often experiencing cloud nine
Only to come crashing down
Landing in this deep, dark, depressive state of mind
Will I ever pull myself from the depths
Hold my heart at even keel
Or am I doomed to this constant tug of war
Never once knowing which side is real

Torri Hebert
3/26/20

# Riddled

What are you doing, Torri
    Have you lost who you are
Remember where you came from
    And how you've come so far
You can't lose yourself
    Or step on that ride again
If you do, all is lost
    Your life, your family, your friends
Don't step back into the darkness
    If you do, you'll lose your light
You're now awakened
    Do you really want to lose your sight
Don't you remember
    How life made you tired
Now you want to wake up
    Because you've been so inspired
If you go back to that life
    You will surely meet your doom
Can't you recall
    How you felt alone in a crowded room
That can't be the life you want
    Can't you feel how your heart is light
No longer carrying the burden
    Or having to put up your toughest fight
You can't want to go back
    When you were blinded by the pain
Your life has become a miracle
    No longer hiding from the shame
The journey of a thousand miles
    Begins with one step
One foot in front of the other
    Not concerned about the rest
Hold your head up high
    As you turn & walk away
If you go back to that lifestyle
    You won't live to see another day
Your chest will become tight
    As you buckle at the knees
If you live that life again
    You'll be riddled with anxiety
Your light is shining now
    You aren't struggling any longer
Your eyes are glistening now
    All the pain has made you stronger

# Riddled

Your life is so full now
      Filled with blessings and hope
Keep on the right path
      And step away from the dope

TORRiLORRi
9/11/2021

# Riddled

What are you doing, Torri
Have you lost who you are
Remember where you came from
And how you've come so far
You can't lose yourself
Or step on that ride again
If you do, all is lost
Your life, your family, your friends
Don't step back into the darkness
If you do, you'll lose your light
You're now awakened
Do you really want to lose your sight
Don't you remember
How life made you tired
Now you want to wake up
Because you've been so inspired
If you go back to that life
You will surely meet your doom
Can't you recall
How you felt alone in a crowded room
That can't be the life you want
Can't you feel how your heart is light
No longer carrying the burden
Or having to put up your toughest fight

# Riddled

You can't want to go back
When you were blinded by the pain
Your life has become a miracle
No longer hiding from the shame
The journey of a thousand miles
Begins with one step
One foot in front of the other
Not concerned about the rest
Hold your head up high
As you turn & walk away
If you go back to that lifestyle
You won't live to see another day
Your chest will become tight
As you buckle at the knees
If you live that life again
You'll be riddled with anxiety
Your light is shining now
You aren't struggling any longer
Your eyes are glistening now
All the pain has made you stronger
Your life is so full now
Filled with blessings & hope
Keep on the right path
And step away from the dope

By: Tokki Tebert
9/16/21

# Wandering Soul

I wonder what it'd be like
    Literally every day
How it might be
    To always feel "okay"
For my entire life
    It has been evident
But I'm sure it doesn't help
    That I've always been so transparent
I've searched for ways to hide
    Put a shield around myself
But it just keeps chipping away
    And can't protect itself
Will I drown from the fear
    Or suffocate from the pain
Maybe choke on the confidence
    That would never let you dance in the rain
I always think about
    When I become gray and old
Will I most regret
    The happiness I couldn't hold
The deck has been stacked against me
    For as long as I know
And I question myself
    Will I make it to 80 years old
My head is loud
    Filled with screams
Of the young girl
    That didn't understand anything
I try to quiet her
    Make her hide away
But I don't always call shots
    When she decides to play
She's screaming in here
    And I'm aching out there
Leaving my soul
    To go nowhere

TORRiLORRi
11/13/2022

# Wandering Soul

Wandering Soul

I wonder what it'd be like
Literally every day
How it might be
To always feel "okay"
For my entire life
It has been evident
But I'm sure it doesn't help
That I've always been so transparent
I've searched for ways to hide
Put a shield around myself
But it just keeps chipping away
And can't protect itself
Will I drown from the fear
Or suffocate from the pain
Maybe choke on the confidence
That would never let you dance in the rain
I always think about
When I become gray & old
Will I most regret
The happiness I couldn't hold
The deck has been against me
For as long as I know
And I question myself
Will I make it to 80 years old
My head is loud
Filled with screams
Of the young girl
That didn't understand anything
I try to quiet her
Make her hide away
But I don't always call shots
When she decides to play
She's screaming in here
And I'm aching out there
Leaving my soul
To go nowhere

By: Torri Hebert
11/13/22

# Elivia

A joyful time
    There was many chatter
Drinking and dancing
    But more the latter
And in you step
    Like a princess off her horse
Instantly they stop
    Because they can feel your force
You radiate happiness
    And giddiness I know
I wish I could harness it
    To let my shine show
You're beautiful and elegant
    And all the pretty things
Every part of myself
    That I don't know about me
Your appearance is left unbotched
    The one time you popped me with your shoe
Looking back now
    You're an angel for all you didn't do
I'll attempt to embody you
    But there's no chance
I'll be even close to your standards
    Or your dance
Know that you're my heart and soul
    And beyond worldly words
Will always meet me in my dreams
    No matter the violent turf
Completely opposite ends of the spectrum
    How different we can be
But that doesn't mean I don't strive to be like you
    A perfect dragonfly, wild and free
I thank God for my days with you
    With coffee and a cigarette
Memories instilled for a life time
    I'm unable to forget
I think of you often
    Now as the days pass faster than before
Praying to my Higher Power often
    Allow me to see her again, I implore
What an impact you've made in the world
    And an impact you've made on this life
When all was lost and I was alone
    You taught me how to fight

# Elivia

There will never be
    An Elivia again, or any other night
Who channels your happiness
    Or shines your light so bright

        TORRiLORRi
        1/16/2023
    Dedicated to Elivia Ramirez "Mawmaw"

# Elivia

A joyful time
There was many chatter
Drinking & Dancing
But more the latter
And in you step
Like a princess off her horse
Instantly they stop
Because they can feel your ~~energy~~ force
You radiate happiness
And giddiness I know
I wish I could harness it
To let my shine show
You're beautiful & elegant
And all the pretty things
Every part of myself
That I don't know about me
Your appearance is left unbotched
The one time you popped me with your shoe
Looking back now
You're an angel for all you didn't do
I'll attempt to embody you
But there's no chance
I'll be even close to your standards
Or your dance

# Elivia

Know that you're my heart & soul
And beyond worldly words
We'll always meet in my dreams
No matter the violent turf
Completely opposite ends of the spectrum
How different we can be
But that doesn't mean I don't strive to be like you
~~A perfect~~ dragonfly, wild & free
I thank God for my days with you
With coffee, and a cigarette
Memories instilled for a life time
I'm unable to forget
I think of you often
Now as the days pass faster than before
Praying to my higher power often
Allow me to see her again, I implore
What an impact you've made in the world
And an impact you've made on this life
When all was lost & I was alone
You taught me how to fight
There will never be
An Elivia on any other night
Who channels your happiness
Or shines your light so bright

By: Torri Lorri
1/16/23
For: Elivia Ramirez "MawMaw"

# Binder

You and I have been through it together
    From the depths of the unseen
Where I hide from it all
    And where I conquer everything
Places most are too scared to go
    Avoiding it like the plague
Places even I cannot fathom
    Nor comprehend, or understand
You've seen all my worst moments
    Listened as I was falling apart
Held my hand through victories too
    You were there from the start
You saw the budding little poet
    Who could rhyme like never before
But at some point, all the pain seeped out
    Landing me on the bathroom floor
Yet here you are again
    Always offering for the words to form
Given our history, it would seem
    We're always running towards the storm
But with every battle fought
    And with every hurricane
Your receiving is always open
    Taking in my pain
Reading the words, looking back now
    On my entire life
The fact that I am still here today
    Is a miraculous sight
The pain has always been there
    The emotions were valid too
Seeing the way my mind's progressed
    From the eyes of a child to an adult's view
I've spent most of my days in sadness
    But you've caught every single throw
Through every phase of my life
    You've never left the show
I know it's amazing, what you'll become
    Not a decrepit binder at all
You'll give hope to the hopeless
    As they read your words in awe
How I wish they understand
    Maybe find some strength too
Hold on for another day
    All because of you

# Binder

Your pages have shown me
    Feelings change between 2 suns
And that some of the battles fought
    Never needed to be won
I'm manifesting you reach them
    All who are lost, outcast, or weird
I believe these words will pass their lips
    And alleviate some of their fears
As I read through you
    Remembering every moment the poem portrayed
How I thought I'd break all apart
    In every moment of those days
But I'm standing here
    Not entirely whole like childhood
But compartmentalized
    To see the grey between the bad and good
And once it becomes a blur to me
    Once the memory fades
How I dream your words live on
    Finally showing what I couldn't say

                        TORRILORRI
                        1/16/2023

# Binder

Binder 1

You & I have been through it together
From the depths of the unseen
Where I hide from it all
And where I conquer everything
Places most are too scared to go
Avoiding it like the plague
Places even I cannot fathom
Nor comprehend, or understand
You've seen all my worst moments
Listened as I was falling apart
Held my hand through victories too
You were there from the start
You saw the budding little poet
Who could rhyme like never before
But at some point, all the pain seeped out
Landing me on the bathroom floor
Yet here you are again
Always offering for the words to form
Given our history, it would seem
We're always running towards the storm
But with every battle fought
And with every hurricane
Your receiving is always opened
Taking in my pain

# Binder

Reading the words, looking back now
On my entire life
The fact that I am still here today
Is a miraculous sight
The pain has always been there
The emotions were valid too
Seeing the way my ~~own~~ minds progressed
From the eyes of a child, to an adults view
I've spent most of my days in sadness
But you've caught every single throw
Through every phase of my life
You've never left the show
I know it's amazing, what you'll become
Not a decrepit binder at all
You'll give hope to the hopeless
As they read your words in awe
How I wish they understand
Maybe finds strength too
Hold on for another day
All because of you
Your pages have shown me
Feelings change between 2 suns
And that some of the battles fought
Never needed to be won

3

I'm manifesting you reach them
All who are lost, outcast, or weird
I believe these words will ~~reach~~ pass ~~their~~ their lips
And aleviate some of ~~their~~ their fears
As I read through you
Remembering every moment the poem portrayed
How I thought I'd break all apart
In every moments of those days
But I'm standing here ~~~~
Not entirely whole like childhood
But compartmentalized
~~Could~~ see the grey between bad & good
And once it becomes a blur to me
Once the memory fades
How I dream your words live on
Finally showing what I couldn't say

By: Torri Lorri
1/16/23

Made in the USA
Columbia, SC
05 June 2024